Remembering:

_____

_____

_____

In Memory Of...

A single life touches many hearts—and together we gather to honor someone truly beloved. As a treasured guest, friend, and family member, please share your thoughts, feelings, and memories in these pages. Write from your heart. Let it say whatever it needs to say, in any way you'd like. Your words will forever be cherished. And know that your presence here means so much.

I carry your heart with me...

– E. E. CUMMINGS –

To love abundantly is to live abundantly,
and to love forever is to live forever.

- HENRY DRUMMOND -

I can look into the world
and see you in every act of love.
Where once you were one,
you are now many.

- MOLLY FUMIA -

There are some who bring a
light so great to the world that
even after they have gone,
the light remains.

- UNKNOWN -

My friends have made the story of my life.

...a life spent loving... is a life well spent.

– SUZANNE CLOTHIER –

Life starts with love and ends with love.

– SANTOSH KALWAR –

If I should ever leave you whom I love
To go along the Silent Way, grieve not.
Nor speak of me with tears, but laugh and talk
Of me as if I were beside you there.

– ISLA PASCHAL RICHARDSON –

Memories need to be shared.

- LOIS LOWRY -

And I will light a candle for you to shatter all
the darkness and bless the times we knew.

– PAUL ALEXANDER –

In the end, it's not the years in your life
that count. It's the life in your years.

We remember best what we love most.

– WARREN GODDARD –

Blessed influence of one true
loving human soul on another!

– GEORGE ELIOT –

Those whom we have loved
never really leave us. They live
on forever in our hearts,
and cast their radiant light
onto our every shadow.

- SYLVANA ROSSETTI -

We are never alone in our grief...

- UNKNOWN -

The ones we love are always in our hearts.

- PROVERB -

I will never forget you even for an interval...

– IZUMI SHIKIBU –

Memories are our greatest inheritance.

– PETER HAMILL –

There are no goodbyes for us.

Thank you for coming into my life
and giving me joy, thank you
for loving me and receiving my love
in return. Thank you for the
memories I will cherish forever.

I leave you love.

— MARY MCLEOD BETHUNE —

In one of the stars I shall be living.
In one of them I shall be laughing.
And so it will be as if all the stars
will be laughing when you look at
the sky at night.

– ANTOINE DE SAINT-EXUPÉRY –

The only lasting beauty is the beauty of the heart.

Looking back over a lifetime, you see
that love was the answer to everything.

— RAY BRADBURY —

Life is a shared experience.

– UNKNOWN –

Through love, through friendship,
a heart lives more than one life...

– ANAÏS NIN –

I am part of all that I have met.

—ALFRED, LORD TENNYSON

The effect of one good-hearted person is incalculable.

– ÓSCAR ARIAS –

Among life's best gifts are the
friends who know and care about us.

– GAYLE LARSON –

...thank you, forever and sincerely...

– ELIZABETH GILBERT –

The memories I value most, I don't ever see them fading.

I remember them always and everywhere...

- ANNA AKHMATOVA -

To live in hearts we leave behind is not to die.

– THOMAS CAMPBELL –

Love is the emblem of eternity: it confounds
all notion of time; effaces all memory of
a beginning, all fear of an end...

– GERMAINE DE STAËL –

Nothing is ever really lost to us as long as we remember it.

- L. M. MONTGOMERY -

...that place in the heart that
holds the measure of your history, the
joy and the grief, the laughter and
the tears, the magic and the wonder; all
the ingredients that add up to the
story of a life well lived.

– LILLI JOLGREN DAY –

All who have been touched by beauty are
touched by sorrow at its passing.

– LOUISE CORDANA –

What the heart remembers most are moments shared.

– ELIZABETH BROWNE –

I embrace you with all my heart.

COMPENDIUM®
live inspired

WITH SPECIAL THANKS TO THE ENTIRE COMPENDIUM FAMILY.

CREDITS:

Written & Compiled by: Miriam Hathaway

Designed by: Jill Labieniec

Edited by: Kristin Eade

ISBN: 978-1-946873-54-5

1st printing. Printed in China with soy and metallic inks.